Riley Road: Navigating the Path to Discover My 6th Great Grandfather, Jacob Riley

BY: HOLLY D. HENDERSON

Riley Road: Navigating the Path to Discover My 6th Great Grandfather, Jacob Riley by Holly D. Henderson

Books may be purchased in quantity from CreateSpace.com, Amazon.com, and BarnesandNoble.com.

Author: Holly D. Henderson, www.TheMessengerMom.com

Cover Design: Kaely Linker, www.KaelyLinker.com

Library of Congress Control Number: 2017909560
CreateSpace Independent Publishing Platform, North Charleston, SC

ISBN: 1545328463
ISBN-13: 978-1545328460

1. Biography & Autobiography, Cultural Heritage
2. Reference, Genealogy, Heraldry

First Edition Printed in the United States

DEDICATION

This book is dedicated to my 2nd great-grandfather, Preston Riley, the son of the white "Judge" and a former black slave woman from Butler, Taylor County, Georgia, and who is the namesake of my 2nd son, Preston Riley Henderson. We can now all rest in peace with the knowledge that this family mystery is finally solved.

CONTENTS

ACKNOWLEDGMENTS

This research is motivated by the desire of relatives past and present to both know and preserve the family legacy of the ancestors of Preston Riley. Thank you, Jennifer Burke, Clinton Ellison, Gloria Ellison, Mildred "Ann" Ellison, Natalie Ellison-Renk, Oscar "Smokey" Ellison, Willi Ellison, Michael Henderson, Makini Lewis, Kaely Linker, Edna E. Lucas, Virginia Martin, Dr. Daniel Merrick, Kaha Fatah Morris, Dr. Nicole Noble, Heather Olsen, Johnny Riley, Sabrina Riley, The Riley family and the Riley-Edwards Family Reunion Committee and Dennis Simpson. I would also like to give special thanks to Karen Janczy and Connie Uy with the Harmony Hall Maryland Chapter of the National Society of Daughters of the American Revolution (NSDAR), and Virginia Crilley of the Taylor County Georgia Historical Society and Rachel Gaydosh (NSDAR) Whidbey Island Oregon Chapter, for their priceless assistance and precious time. I am also grateful to my peers who reviewed this work and gave meaningful advice.

HOLLY HENDERSON

CHAPTER 1: STARTING THE JOURNEY

Your word is a lamp for my feet, a light on my path.

– Psalm 119:105

When embarking on any journey, whether an actual road trip with young children or a trip down memory lane with loved ones, certain items are needed, and dare I say, indispensable, to have with you along the way. These precious items include: driving directions, an updated GPS or good old Atlas, a full tank of fuel (both literally and figuratively), energy for driving or being co-navigator, sustenance (earthly and spiritual), money (usually more than what you've planned to spend), patience (lots of it), a good dose of humor (mixed with a healthy dose of irritability) and time: time to drive to your destination, to reflect, to rest, to enjoy the journey, to return home, and to have a vacation from your vacation.

As a former domestic and international flight attendant at Continental Airlines, Inc. for seven years, I have seen and experienced many seasoned and novice travelers; some solo, and others were with loved ones, especially young children. I am always amazed at the skilled mothers who navigate the narrow aisles of an aircraft with carry-on luggage, purses, diaper bags, coats, and a baby in a sling with a toddler in tow. Many times, these brave mothers are traveling alone with all this gear for hours. I was amazed at their adeptness to manage the situation. Ultimately, they did what had to be done to achieve their goal: to arrive at their destination, alive, although, not necessarily in one (mental) piece.

After the events of 9/11, I decided to keep my feet on the ground. I was eventually hired as a gubernatorial appointee by the administration of Robert E. Ehrlich (the first Republican Governor in Maryland in more than 42 years). I was selected to be the Deputy Director of Communications at the Baltimore Washington International Airport (BWI) under the Maryland Aviation Administration (MAA) a division of the Maryland Department of Transportation (MDOT).

I served as liaison to the media, wrote press releases and speeches, and planned events during a multi-million-dollar renovation and expansion at BWI. This timeframe included, the renaming of BWI to "Thurgood Marshall Baltimore Washington International Airport" to honor the late African-American Supreme Court Justice. I also had the pleasure of coordinating the arriving flight and subsequent event at the U.S. Capitol to honor the adored Civil Rights leader, Ms. Rosa Parks.

Two weeks later, I would serve in a new position as Director of Communications for MDOT's Maryland Transit Administration (MTA) located in downtown Baltimore. The MTA is "one of the largest multi-modal transit systems in the United States" (as of May 2, 2017, according to its website). Throughout this time, I was working on my Masters of Science in Engineering/Transportation Management at Morgan State University. In 2006, I wrote a thesis entitled "*The Impact of 9/11 on Airport Security Systems: A Case Study of Baltimore/Washington International Airport*". A three-hour defense of the thesis resulted in its publication.

I know firsthand about travelling via trains, planes, and automobiles. I have taken and endured road trips for business and pleasure. According to an old MySpace Survey, I have travelled over 11% of the world! It wasn't until my marriage in 2006 and having my first son a year later during the week of our first anniversary, that I really started the journey of researching my family tree. That genetic and emotional pull to unearth the roots of one's family tree became, and still is to this day, insatiable! My journey of navigating the information to find my lost (and found) maternal and paternal ancestors began earnestly in 2007.

My dear mother, Mildred "Ann" (Jackson) Ellison, an English and Communications professor, has for my entire life relayed the family history as it was handed down to her from generations past, as seems to be the custom of the family matriarchs. I listened, not fully understanding all the information and nodded lovingly as I listened to her over the years.

My dear father, Willi Ellison, a federal law enforcement officer, was born near Munich, Germany to a black U.S. Army soldier, William Ellison, and a white German citizen, Gertrud Ulbrich, shortly after the end of World War II. My dad immigrated to the U.S.A. when he was 10 years old. He was reared in the Mid-West not knowing too much about either his maternal or paternal family lines.

In 2009, with the advent of using the Internet for research, and specifically signing up with a free account on *Ancestry.com*, I called my Mom to again ask for the family history to insert into the online *Ancestry.com* family tree. I realized upon seeing the names on the various tree branches, that I was a visual learner and finally began to reconcile the oral family history with the visual names listed on the tree. Then, I earnestly began using the famous green hint leaves and my "Maclin" family tree began to take shape.

Little did I know, in those early days of researching hints and interviewing family members for information, that my initial maternal "Maclin" tree would become my catch-all tree for both maternal and paternal family information. As I began to enter my paternal Riley-Ellison information, the locked mysteries of hidden information began to open and to unveil previously unknown details about the family. It is this unlocked information that started the engine of my vehicle of knowledge down *Riley Road: Navigating the Path to Discover My 6th Great Grandfather, Jacob Riley.*

Ironically, the road for Riley-Ellison roots had begun on a road trip from Maryland to Florida in the mid-1970s. My mother was eager to meet the Ellison family upon hearing about cousins, aunts, and uncles in Georgia. My father's great uncle, Clinton Riley and "Auntie" Ora Lee graciously hosted our family when we visited Jacksonville. Uncle Riley, (known also as "Uncle Honey" or "Papa Shank") as my family called him, is the son of Preston Riley. Uncle Honey and Auntie directed my parents from the backseat of their car driven by my dad. This road tour of Butler, Georgia, included a drive-by of Preston's property, nestled not too far from the Five Corners area near *the* Riley Road, literally.

The trip to Butler and Thomaston, Georgia, yielded a harvest of relatives. My late grandfather, William Clifford "W.C." Ellison, was one of four brothers: Uncle "Sonny" Ellison, Uncle Sanders Key "S.K." Ellison, and Uncle Richard "Dick" Ellison. Their wives and children were a delightful mix of interesting personalities.

My mother recalls writing names and dates observed on headstones in the cemetery behind Antioch Missionary Baptist Church. She quizzed my father on the various names as Uncle Riley skillfully guided our family through the Riley-Ellison territory. Our family grew exponentially in a matter of days and we are eternally grateful to be linked with them.

In the interim of inserting information onto my online family tree, I began to read various blogs and books on researching your family history and using "genetic genealogy":[1] the combination of using DNA test results to solve some genealogical research mysteries and unveil long-lost relatives. Intrigued, I began this method of genetic genealogy, where my Dad, Willi Ellison, and I began to take a series of various DNA (Y-DNA,[2] mt-DNA,[3] at-DNA)[4] tests with DNA testing companies including *DNA*

---

[1] *"International Society of Genetic Genealogy,"* website, *ISOGG.org,* (https://isogg.org/wiki/Genetic_genealogy : accessed 2 May 2017, describes how using DNA testing along with traditional historical documented evidence to infer the relationship between individuals.

[2] *"International Society of Genetic Genealogy,"* accessed 2 May 2017, https://isogg.org/wiki/Genetic_genealogy, description of why using a Y-DNA test of the male-only Y Chromosome is typically used in surname research and those results are collated within surname DNA projects (i.e. Riley, Smith).

[3] *"International Society of Genetic Genealogy,"* accessed 2 May 2017, https://isogg.org/wiki/Genetic_genealogy, description of why using an mt-DNA test of the Mitochondria; a male can take both Y-DNA and an mt-DNA tests as mt-DNA is passed down from mother to child, regardless of gender; whereas, a female child does not carry the Y-DNA chromosome and thus is able to take the male-only test; mt-DNA testing involves sequencing or testing the HVR-1 region, HVR-2 region or both.

[4] *"International Society of Genetic Genealogy,"* accessed 2 May 2017, https://isogg.org/wiki/Genetic_genealogy, details an Autosomal or at-DNA test; humans have one pair of sex chromosomes (X chromosome and the Y chromosome) and 22 pairs of autosomes; it is impossible to know from at-DNA testing which ethnic breakdown of data comes from the maternal or paternal line; it is like taking various ingredients to bake a cake, one cannot

Consultants, Family Tree DNA, and AncestryDNA.

According to my 2016 *AncestryDNA* at-DNA results, my estimated ethnicity is 59% "Africa" (with a regional breakdown of: Ivory Coast/Ghana, 19%; Benin/Togo 16%; Cameroon/Congo, 12%; Nigeria, 5%) and 41% "Europe" (with a regional breakdown of: Ireland, 10%; Europe East, 8%; Great Britain, 7%; Scandinavia, 6%). In comparison, my 2015 Family Tree Family Finder DNA at-DNA results show: 60% "Africa" to 40% "European" (with a higher regional European breakdown of Eastern Europe, 21%; British Isles, 15%; and Scandinavia 4%). Either way, luckily my Riley roots reshuffled enough for me to rock out to U2 (my favorite 80's band) and long to wear woolen sweaters as I dream of returning one-day to visit the rolling hills and vales of green on the lovely "Emerald Isle."

Unfortunately, I did not find the DNA information that I wanted about my father's paternal-maternal Riley line because my father's paternal grandmother, Lovenia, who was a daughter of Preston Riley, would not yield me the Y-DNA that is passed down from father to son, from generation to generation. If Lovenia had been a male, keeping the male surname via bloodline, then I could have received the coveted Riley Y-DNA results that I needed.

So, the quest for more details on the Riley history continued down a winding path of whose destination was yet unknown.

What information to me was known, had been compiled and collected since the first Riley Family Reunion in 1970. The following Riley History[5] was printed (and is used here with permission from the Riley-Edwards Family and Reunion Committee) in the booklet for the 2015 Riley-Edwards Family Reunion held in St. Augustine, Florida.

---

tell that the cup of sugar represents your maternal line and the cup of flour represents your paternal line.

[5] Riley-Edwards Family History, Riley-Edwards Family Reunion program, St. Augustine, Florida, 2015, used with permission.

OUR FAMILY HISTORY

RILEY History

The first ancestor we have information about is Nettie or Neddie Riley. (According to Mother's [Aunt Florence's] hand written notes, the name is Nellie.) We have no information concerning her parents or siblings, but we do know that she was a slave born sometime in the early 1800s. She worked as a washwoman and lived on a plantation in Taylor County, Georgia. She gave birth to at least two children, Hannah and Nellie, who were born enslaved. Hannah and Nellie were also given the surname Riley. There is no information about their father nor is there any additional information regarding Nellie.

Hannah Riley (b. 1819) had two children that we know of: Sallie (b. 1848 – d. 09 Nov 1934) and Jeff (b. between 1840 and 1850). They were both born in Taylor County, GA and both were enslaved and given the surname Riley. (Additional children, according to Mother's notes: Mary Colbert wife of Wilburn Colbert and Caroline McCrary wife of Walsh McCrary). At the age of 12, Sallie was separated from the other slaves, became a "house girl", and worked for the slave master in the house. She was given the name "Mammy Sallie." Sallie married former slave John Mangham 19 Jan, 1908 and together they had one son, John, who died at an early age from injuries sustained from a fire.

Mammy Sallie gave birth to four sons with the Riley surname: Dink (b. 1860)[6], Preston (b 1868 – d. 30 Oct 1957), Sanders "Key" (b. 1870) and Clinton (b. 1875). Their father

---

[6] "1910 United States Federal Census," database, *Ancestry.com*, (http://www.ancestry.com : accessed 28 April 2016), entry for Dick Riley, age 46, mulatto, Carsonville, Taylor County, Georgia; Roll: T624_209; Page: 8A; Enumeration District: 0117; FHL microfilm: 1374222 ; citing United States of America, Bureau of the Census; Thirteenth Census of the United States, 1910; (NARA microfilm publication T624, 1,178 rolls); Records of the Bureau of the Census, Washington, D.C. It appears that William Clifton or W.C. is nicknamed "Dink" Riley. Dink is also enumerated as being Mulatto in the 1920 Carsonville, Taylor Co, GA census.

was believed to be Thomas J. Riley, a man of Irish descent, who owned the Riley Plantation, was a judge, as well as the Mayor of the City of Butler, Georgia (Taylor County) for which he helped name the city.

The Riley's migrated to Georgia from Ireland's Shannon Valley and, apparently after a family dispute, the surname was changed from O'Reilly to Riley. The O'Reilly's and Reilly's are the descendants of the Gaelic Irish sept, the O'Raghailligh of Breffny and whose influence extended to counties Cavan, Westmeath and Langford. The O'Reilly's were such a powerful influence, that at one stage in their reign of power that issued their own coinage. The Riley maxim (including variants O'Reilly and O'Reily) is "Fortitundine et Prudentia," which means "With Fortitude and Prudence," while the name itself means "brave."

Preston "Pa Press" Riley married Judy Searcy (some records call her Judie and some call her Julia) on 03 Jan 1889 in Taylor County. Judy/Julia/Judie/Juda was probably born in May 1868, based on [U.S. Federal] Census data. Her parents were Thomas and Melvinia "Vinny" Searcy. Melvinia's maiden name was Buford. Thomas and Melvinia were married September 28, 1868 in Taylor County, Georgia. Thomas, Vinny and their children appear in both the 1870 and 1880 censuses in Taylor County. Judy had an older brother, Thomas, who married Lucile Baldwin on April 1, 1894, and an older brother Samuel who married Mollie Searcy on July 29, 1888 (both marriages in Taylor Co.). Judy also had several younger siblings (names unknown).

Preston and Judy had 11 children: William Clifton (b. 09 Jun 1887 – d. 19 Apr 1968), Cleveland ("Cleve" b. Jan 1889 – d. 1986), Sanders (b. Dec 1891 – d. Feb 1968), Elmyra ("Myra" Searcy (b. 1892), Louvenia (b 05 Jan 1895 – d. [1961]), twins Henry Clay ("Fox") (b. Dec 1898 - d. 24 Nov 1969) and Jessie M. (b. Dec 1898 – 12 Jul 1970), Eury D. ("Dick) (b. 10 May 1894 – d. 04 Jan 1981), Dudley Hugh Riley (b. 1907), Florence ("Aunt Tump") (b. 16 Nov 1904 – d. 14 May 2003), Clinton ("Honey/Unc/Uncle Clint/Shank") (b. 08 Sep 1908 – d. 13 Feb 1991 and was married to his cousin

Ora Lee McCrary).

William Clifton Douglas Riley married Lydie and they no children. Cleveland "Cleve" had five children: Ernestine, Jessie, Kathleen, Tommie, and Sanders "Key". Sanders "Key" married Ressie and they had seven children (and lived in Griffin, GA, called "Riley Quarters"): Thurmond, Quiller, Naomi, Ruth, Beatrice ("Essie Bea"), Eury ("Bish") and Arthur. Elmyra Searcy had thirteen children: Addis, Albert, Carrie, Clark, Eddie Frances (who died at birth), George, James Curtis, Johnny B., Laney, M.T., Mack, Nathaniel and Oscar.

Louvenia Riley married John Ellison from Buena Vista, Georgia. They had four sons: Richard ("Uncle Dick"), Sanders Key ("Uncle SK"), Riley ("Uncle Sonny"), and William Clifford ("WC"/ "Ralph"). [John Ellison was given then nickname "Riley".] After John Ellison died on July 2, 1921, in Shiglar, GA (Worth County) at 28 years old from an infection, Pa Press raised his youngest three grandsons, as Louvenia (Riley) Ellison moved and settled in Cleveland, Ohio. John Ellison, also called
"Riley Ellison", later in life is the son of Rube Ellison. Before John joined the Army on April 3, 1895, during WWI, he worked as a farmhand for Mr. R.C. Garrett in Shiglar, GA. There is not a lot of additional information on the history of John Ellison. Jessie married Lizzy Mae and they had one child named Thomas, also known as "Bum." Eury had two children: Goodman and Lucille.

Florence married Charlie West Edwards and they had 10 children (see Edward's family history). Clinton married Ora Lee McCrary and they had no children.

EDWARDS History

What we know of the Edwards' family history begins with Berry and Susie Edwards who also lived in Butler (Taylor County), Georgia and had four children: Jim, Nettie, Charlotte, and Charlie. Charlie married Laura Dugger and they had four children: Gene, Charlie West, Berry, and Bessie. After the passing of Laura, Charlie married Vesta

(Big Mama) and they had four children: Cary, Mamie, Cora, and Mitchell (Uncle Bud).

Gene married Lula Thomas and they had five sons: Tommy, Eugene, Charles, Jimmy and Ralph. Bessie married Essie Riley who is believed to be related to our branch of the Rileys. Berry married Jeffie Callaway and they had two children: Clara Mae Edwards-Evans and Berry, Jr. Cary was married, his wife and children's names are unknown now.

Mamie was married but her husband's name is unknown now. They had one son named Mitchell Edwards.

Cora was married to Charlie Smith, they had no children.

Mitchell (Uncle Bud) was married, although his wife's name is unknown, they had five children: Grace, Blanche, and the other three children's names are unknown.

Charlie West Edwards (Grandson of Berry Edwards) married Florence Riley, who was the daughter of Preston "Pa Press" and Judy (Searcy) Riley. They had ten children: Lyrica, Eunice ("Sister"), Mary Emma, William, Aurelia ("Lil Sister"), Edna, Clinton, Linwood ("Roebuck"), Virginia, and Corley.

The following information is an update from the 2015 Riley-Edwards Reunion booklet.

The 1870 U.S. Census, Taylor County, Georgia, lists a Jackson Riley in the household of Hannah. Jackson's relationship to Hannah is unknown. Hannah Riley apparently had also had two additional children: Mary (Riley) Colbert (b. 1844 in Butler, GA) and daughter Caroline (b. 1849 in Butler, GA). (In addition to the four sons of Mammy Sallie named in the 2015 booklet, two more children have been found according to a Freedmen's Bureau Ordinary Court record in 1865: Tim, born in 1863, and William, born in 1849.[7]   However, the year of William's birth as being recorded as 1849, would make Sallie (born in 1848) only one year old: too young to birth her own child. Thus, it is more likely that this William is Sallie's younger brother with shared mother Hannah.

Sanders "Key" apparently owned a store named "Riley Market" which was the first black-owned grocery store in Griffin, GA. There, he sold cured meats from bulls he had raised, and made money from an apartment building that he owned and rented out. Sanders "Key" was digging in an attempt to fix a gas leak/gasoline when the line burst. He suffered third-degree burns and died of his injuries.

Thurmond Riley, the son of Sanders "Key" and Ressie, is the grandfather to Kelvin Riley, Gail, and Teri. Uncle S.K. married China Doll. Another nickname for William Clifford ("WC") Ellison, was "Ralph."

The first-ever Riley Family Reunion was held in 1979[8] at Antioch Missionary Baptist Church.[9] My paternal Great Aunt

---

[7] "1880 United States Federal Census," database, *Ancestry.com*, (http://www.ancestry.com : accessed 28 April 2016), entry for Hannah Riley, age 61, black, Carsonville, Taylor County, Georgia; Roll: 166; Family History Film: 1254166; Page: 81B; Enumeration District: 076; Image: 0784; citing 1880 U.S. Census Index provided by The Church of Jesus Christ of Latter-day Saints. Hannah is enumerated in the same household (with the children listed in Clifton Riley's will): William Clifton Riley, age 16; Preston Riley age 12; and Sanders Key Riley age 10. It appears that William Clifton or W.C. is nicknamed "Dink" Riley; It should be noted that this William is not the same child as William "Dink" Clifton or W.C. Riley; and could not be located after this date. The age of Tim Riley matches that of William Clifton "Dink" Riley; Tim could also not be found in further research.

[8] See Appendix A, Vintage 1979 Riley Reunion Program Cover.

[9] Antioch Baptist Church was founded in 1829 and began receiving slaves into its membership. The church went into decline during the Civil War years and by 1867 many costly repairs were needed. In 1869, the church was organized into Antioch Missionary Baptist Church (for the people of color, while the white membership merged with other churches); the church cemetery is where many Riley relatives are buried, including the author's paternal Grandfather, William C. Ellison. Taylor Co Family Churches; Database, *Rootsweb;* http://www.rootsweb.ancestry.com/~gataylor/antibp.htm : 2017; citing,

Florence (Riley) Edwards McHelen[10] was on a quest in the late
1960s, like mine, to find the first name of her white paternal
grand-father, "The Judge" [Riley] of Taylor County, Georgia. No
one in the family knew the first name of Judge Riley, only that he
was the father of Preston Riley. The black Rileys and the white
Rileys are Taylor County openly (at least, to an extent) of their
kinship from Butler, Taylor County. Knowing this, Aunt Florence
reached out to Frank Riley, son of the late Judge, Harley Riley, to
inquire information, in writing, on "The Judge". Frank Riley
responded with a handwritten letter to Florence, but fell short of
openly stating in writing the familial relationship or answering her
question to the first name of her grandfather.

This is a transcription[11] of a letter written from Frank Riley to
Florence McHelen (daughter of Preston Riley),[12] Taylor County,
Georgia (and is used with permission by Mrs. Edna E. Lucas):

They Tarried in Taylor a Georgia County by Essie Jones Childs; Warner:
Central Georgia Genealogical Society, 1992.

[10] "1910 United States Federal Census," database, *Ancestry.com.*
(http://www.ancestry.com : accessed 28 April 2016), entry for Florence
Riley, age 5, Carsonville, Talbot County, Georgia; Roll: T624_209; Page: 5A;
Enumeration District: 0117; FHL microfilm: 1374222; citing Thirteenth
Census of the United States, 1910 (NARA microfilm publication T624, 1,178
rolls), Records of the Bureau of the Census, Record Group 29, National
Archives, Washington, D.C.; Florence (Riley) Edwards McHelen, was born
circa 1905. She is a daughter of Preston Riley and Judy/Julia (Searcy) Riley.
Florence is the younger sister to my great grandmother, Louvenia (Riley)
Ellison.

[11] "1940 United States Federal Census," database, *Ancestry.com,*
(http://www.ancestry.com : accessed 28 April 2016), entry for Frank Riley,
age 17, white, Butler, Taylor County, Georgia; Roll: T627_711; Page: 7A;
Enumeration District: 133-5; citing United States of America, Bureau of the
Census; Sixteenth Census of the United States, 1940; Washington, D.C.:
National Archives and Records Administration, 1940; T626. Frank Montfort
Riley was the son of Olivia (Montfort) and Judge Harley Riley and is listed
with his father in the 1940 Butler, Taylor Co, Ga census Letter to Florence
Riley McHelen, daughter of Preston Riley from Frank Riley; the great
nephew of Thomas Jefferson Riley and the 2nd great-grandson of Jacob
Riley, Revolutionary War Patriot – dated July 14, 1979.

[12] See Appendix B, Original letter from Frank Riley to Florence (Riley)
Edwards McHelen, circa 1979.

Sunday, July 14, 1979

To: Florence McHelen (daughter of Press Riley Taylor County, Georgia)

Dear Florence -

I enjoyed the visit over the telephone with you Sunday recalling the days of the lifetime of your father Preston Riley.

I have fond memories of him as I was a young boy at that time. I still think of him and his family often as I pass the home site on my way to Thomaston, Georgia overlooking the beautiful Flint River. It was located right at the Flint River bridge on the Taylor County side on US Highway 19 in the northern part of the County.

I can remember what the house where you lived as a child look like as if I had seen it this morning. It was a house with a front porch all the way across the front with the board and batten planks running up and down the outside.

There was plenty of open land around the house for the growing of crops and vegetables, as your father was a good provider for his family.

You can tell all your children, grandchildren, great-grandchildren, and great-great grandchildren that they have a good heritage, as the Riley clan were well respected and were good solid citizens in the community.

Press Riley was quite a character and I have fond memories of him as a young boy and happy summer days here on the farm where I live now on a high bluff overlooking the Flint River (about 2 miles up the river from your former home).

Press had a good sense of humor and didn't ever seem to "meet a stranger".

He likes to grow things and I remember my father, Harley Riley, asking him one day at the end of corn harvest season if he had made a good corn crop and he immediately answered, "I made so much corn that I had to move it off the field to stack it." He never lacked for an answer!

*Press thought a lot of my father and we all thought a lot
of him. He liked to walk (as there were very few cares), and
about this time of the year when his crop "was laid by" and
our crop too, we would look up and would see press coming
to visit us on the farm and we would have a pleasant visit
and "catch up on all the news" in the community. He would
then visit throughout the community.*

*I remember Judy his wife and she was a great support
to him and the rest of the family. A man can only do so much
for his family, but it takes the support of the good wife and
mother, and she was this to her family.*

*Press lived through the Depression years of the 1920s
and 30s when nobody had much money but the people on the
farm fared better than those in cities and that "pace of life"
was much slower in those days, which you and I agreed on
the telephone. We could use some of that in today's living!*

*I wish I had a snapshot picture, but no one took any
pictures in those days, I remember his brothers Keith,[13]
Clinton and others Fox Riley, [14]Doug Riley,[15] Howard Riley,
Jess Riley,[16] Will Riley, & Homer Riley,[17] all good friends of
ours. Some of them were farmers and others were in the
timber industry.*

---

[13]The letter is written from a first-hand account. It seems that when Frank
writes "his brother Keith," he is referring to Preston's brother Sanders Key.

[14] In the notes of Aunt Florence, she refers to "Fox" Riley as "Uncle Fox," a
nickname, as no Fox Riley can be found in any census record.

[15] It is not clear in this letter if this Doug Riley is the same person as
Preston's son or another Riley relation.

[16] Another of Preston's sons is Jess Riley, who is enumerated in the 1910
census with his father and his grandmother, Sallie, and is listed as Black.

[17] "1860 United States Federal Census," database, *Ancestry.com*,
(http://www.ancestry.com : accessed 28 April 2016), entry for Martin H.
Riley, age 16, Militia District 768, Taylor County, Georgia; Roll: M653_137;
Page: 123; Image: 329; Family History Library Film: 803137; 1860 U.S.
census, population schedule. NARA microfilm publication M653, 1,438 rolls.
Washington, D.C.: National Archives and Records. Martin "Homer" Riley, is
the white son of Harriet (Howe) and Thomas Jefferson Riley. Homer and his
father are enumerated in the 1860 Taylor Co, GA census.

Well, Florence, I hope this gives your folks a picture of your father's life and the times in which he lived.[18]

Hope this finds you well and enjoy your family reunion.

Sincerely,

Frank Riley (Son of Harley Riley)

While the letter did not provide the obvious information desired (that about Frank Riley acknowledging his kinship to Preston), it wasn't until March 2017, in identifying names and relationships of persons (specifically the brothers of Preston Riley) mentioned by Frank Riley at the end of his letter and reconciling that information with persons on my family tree, did some hidden information become apparent. Frank Riley had provided important clues connecting the black and white Riley families from Butler, Taylor County, Georgia:

I wish I had a snapshot picture, but no one took any pictures in those days, I remember his brothers Keith, Clinton and others Fox Riley, Doug Riley, Howard Riley, Jess Riley, Will Riley, & Homer Riley, all good friends of ours. Some of them were farmers and others were in the timber industry.

Keith, Clinton, Fox, Doug, Howard, Jess and Will Riley were all black brothers or relatives of Preston. However, Martin "Homer" Riley (b. 24 Dec 1844 – d. 03 Jul 1911, Butler, Taylor County, Georgia) was the white son of "The Judge" and his wife Harriet (Howe) Riley.[19] Thus, making Homer and Preston half-brothers.

---

[18] Frank Riley was an adult upon the death of Preston Riley. Frank lived during the lifetime of Preston's children.

[19] "1860 United States Federal Census," database, *Ancestry.com,* (http://www.ancestry.com : accessed 28 April 2016), entry for Homer Riley, age 71, Militia District 768, Taylor County, Georgia; Roll: M432_83; Page: 123; Image: 148; citing Original data, 1850 United States Federal Census; Eighth Census of the United States, 1860; (National Archives Microfilm Publication M432, 1009 rolls); Records of the Bureau of the Census, Washington, D.C.

In researching the ancestry and descendants of Preston Riley, I was blessed to know my cousin Edna (Edwards) Lucas better through phone interviews and written correspondence. She has a sharp mind and is quick-witted. Edna is one of the oldest surviving grandchildren of Preston. Edna is the daughter of Aunt Florence whose sister was Louvenia (Riley) Ellison, my deceased great-grandmother that I never knew.

In fact, I have never even seen a picture of my great-grandmother. Out of all of Preston's 11 children, Louvenia had remained another family mystery until revelations of her life became unveiled on this "Riley Road" excursion in 2017. Upon the death of her mother, Florence, Edna took possession of some of these notes and memorabilia. This vast collection of memorabilia dates back to the first Riley Family Reunion in 1979 until present. Edna mailed me a large box of past reunion programs, letters, and photographs.

The following transcriptions are from the diary of Florence (Riley) McHelen (daughter of Preston Riley) and are used with permission from Mrs. Edna E. Lucas.[20]

---

[20] Hand written family notes in after 1980 by Florence Riley McHelen, daughter of Preston Riley; first transcription February 14, 1982 and July 31, 1982. These family notes and Frank Riley's letter became the basis of the first Riley reunion held in 1979. The information collected by Aunt Florence can be verified by contemporary records. Aunt Florence provides details in her family notes[20] regarding the family of Preston Riley, including the identification of "The Judge" with Sallie Riley.

7-31- [19]82

Jeff Riley white man[21]

Sally Riley – land Sally gave me were sold to Riley

Hannah was Sally's mom[22]

Sally was Pa Press' mom. At age 12 years old she was pulled from among the other slaves, as one of the best girls to be a house girl. Mama Sally at age 12 years old went to work for a lady named Mrs. Nick. Mama Sally [would] cook, house cleaning, sewing, crochet and made canvas that would cover a wagon (like the ones they show on the TV now). She also made bonnets with long tail and George Washington's bonnet. She had many talents. Mrs. Nick traveled and those covered wagons, long dresses and bonnets.

At age 13, Mama Sally got pregnant and thought she were swollen. Her master Mrs. Nick told her she had swallowed a pumpkin seed. So, when her Neddie got a chance to talk with her, she had taken Mammie Sally to the side [and] explained to her she was going to have a baby. Mrs. Nick mama Sally's master kept her children while she worked. Preston was born just after slavery ended. Clinton and Key were born about two years after slavery ended.

Jeff had a brother named Nelson, he was a very mean man, and in slavery they use to feed the family like they were hogs with a trough with no silverware in the yard. And when Nelson would get mad, he would spit in the food and grab a handful and throw it at the other slaves just to mess up all the food, and they wouldn't get any more food to eat, but had

---

[21] Aunt Florence provides details in her family notes regarding the family of Preston Riley, including the later identification of "The Judge" named "Jeff" with Sallie Riley.

[22] "1870 United States Federal Census," database, *Ancestry.com.* (http://www.ancestry.com : accessed 28 April 2016), entry for Hannah Riley, Prattsburg, Talbot County, Georgia; citing National Archives microfilm publication M593_175; Page: 91B; Image: 186; Family History Library Film: 545674; Hannah is the mother of Sallie and she appears in the 1870 Prattsburg, Talbot Co, GA census, enumerated with Sarah Riley (Sallie), Dink Riley, Preston Riley and Key Riley.

to work when they didn't have much food to eat from the beginning.

Uncle Nelson fed [ate] out in yard in [on a] tray – in slavery and [would] get mad and civil and cross

and get hand full of meal [food from the tray] and throw it in the face of a 12-year-old house girl.

2-14- [19]82

Miss Nick [would] make covers [for] wagon – say Dink was six years old when slavery ended.

"CIVIL WAR IN THE RILEY FAMILY"

I read this letter in 1979 at the first family reunion at Antioch Baptist Church. Many people in the church remembered this civil war, some of them were sitting in the front row.

Uncle Key have always saved money. The oldest Riley's have always had money but nobody knows where the money came from. Sometimes they would have 5lb sacks of money that the kept in the house.

Uncle Key bought a large track of land in Carsonville, GA. He bought the house from Mr. Monk, the man Mama Sallie worked for as a cook.[23] Mr. Monk got mad at Uncle Key ripped his shirt and called him a Nigger because Mr. Monk wanted the house back: it was a nice plantation. This is what started the fight.

In the year of 1886 Carsonville, [GA] whites and blacks were shooting each other [mini civil war].

---

[23] "1880 United States Federal Census," database, *Ancestry.com*, (http://www.ancestry.com : accessed 28 April 2016), entry for Sallie Riley, age 32, black, Carsonville, Taylor County, Georgia; Roll: 166; Page: 81B; Image: 784; Family History Library Film: 1254166; Enumeration District: 076; citing 1870 U.S. census, population schedules; NARA microfilm publication. Sallie Riley is enumerated in 1880, with the S.S. Monk household #140 (who was also mentioned in the notes of Florence) is listed as age 33, Black, and a Cook.

A lot of people from the [Florida panhandle] about 35-45 miles away [both white and black] came to help Uncle Key in this fight against Mr. Monk.

The white man named John Riley[24] furnished him with shells [ammo and] guns. Julia was six months pregnant with one of her children and sat with Key [Riley's] wife and Grandma Julia in the chimney all night during the shoot-out. Dink Riley was 14 years old and said when the guns would get hot, he would dunk them in a barrel of water to cool the guns off. Charlie W. Edwards' uncle was Rev. Jackson. He assisted in this civil war too.

Key shot one white man, Mr. Monk [the cook who Julia Riley worked for] in the shoulder. When Mr. Monk was shot all the shooting stopped.

My uncle Fox stated years ago that they made moonshine and sold it to the state capital to the governor's office. They always had a little store or [were] running a sawmill and worked for themselves.

"VOTES COUNTING IN THE 1886"

Uncle Dink, Uncle Clint and Uncle Key were the only three (3) people that could count the votes and [white people] called them "paddy's" and they called the other colored folks (and all dark complexion people) "Niggers". Uncle Dink was 14 years old in 1886. Their granddaddy was the Judge and he had them count the votes, only them.[25]

---

[24] "1870 United States Federal Census," database, *Ancestry.com*, (http://www.ancestry.com : accessed 28 April 2016), entry for John C. Riley, age 37, white, Wilkinson, Talbot County, Georgia; Roll: M593_175; Page: 43B; Image:.352422; Family History Library Film: 545674; citing 1870 U.S. census, population schedules; NARA microfilm publication M593, 1,761 rolls; Washington, D.C.: National Archives and Record Administration.

This researcher believes that this John Riley is the son of John P. Riley and grandson of John Riley from Orange County, North Carolina, who served in the Revolutionary War. This would make John Riley a cousin of Preston Riley, my 2nd Great Grandfather. Both White and Black Rileys in Taylor/Talbot County, GA, openly acknowledge their kinship.

[25] "Georgia, Returns of Qualified Voters and Reconstruction Oath Books, 1867-1869." Database. *Ancestry.com*, http://www.ancestry.com : 2016.

Nelson Gray was the first servant [deacon?] of Antioch.

CHAPTER 2: MAPPING IT OUT

When preparing for a road trip that may take you cross-country, it is helpful to know where you are going. It is wise to use an updated GPS or map providing you with essential directions to your desired destination. The same holds true for mapping out your genealogical research. A savvy explorer prepares for all driving conditions: bright headlights to see where you are going, a flashlight to shine the light of truth on interior knowledge, putting the vehicle in the right gear to climb the mountain of information one has collected, driving slowly through the muddy puddles of unclear data, and changing to snow tires for icy roads and cold-call conversations as you cross the tough terrain of controversial findings.

The latest tech equipment and gadgets can aid your genealogy research. Psychologically preparing yourself for the finding or lack of finding desired documents is also crucial. One is never fully prepared for the "ah-ha" moments, or the acceptance of defeat that a piece of evidence is probably in a stranger's attic, has not been digitized to be found on Google, or worse, that the "smoking gun" document is non-existent.

One can call "shot gun" to ride in the front row to experience the thrill of the research journey, only to be relegated to the back of the bus because they refused to believe that their family tree on *Ancestry.com* might be inaccurate and thus leading others down a dead-end road. Some researchers will not put their "car" of facts in reverse to head down another road of promising information. No, they will sit in their car for days, weeks, years even, because the fear of not finding the finish line is too great and their oil tank of emotional energy has run dry.

If one truly wants to map out a path of research successfully, they must first encounter and conquer the highway of the mind and believe the pinnacle of success is one mile closer today than it was yesterday. Crossing the rickety old wooden bridge of historical documents to reach the new world-wide-web of the internet highway of information is scary indeed. The one piece of paper that you need to register your findings is not in the glovebox of your car when you need it most. No one likes being side-swiped by misinformation on the Internet. Or waiting for the "Good Samaritan" to arrive; much damage can be done by ignoring information passed on from generation to generation.

I needed a plan to map out my journey on this Riley Road. In some ways today, this Riley Road still leads to the dusty Georgia red clay dirt roads. The path was a spiraling trail into Butler. The dusty Georgia roads led me to heavily populated red-clay regions of Taylor County. I recall the tasty Brunswick Stew simmering in the outdoor black potbelly kettle over an open fire made proudly by "Uncle S.K.", Grandad's older brother.

It is hard in life, mind and spirit to find one's way home, when one lives a good 13-hour drive from the homestead. Will I remember the names of my distant cousins or who is who, when I arrive years later? Will I find that the folks I had remembered are long since passed and new faces have emerged? What will I find after 20 years?

My mind raced to the family reunion in Miami when I was 10 years old. Grandad was with us. Now, I am a mother with a ten-year-old son. I have also a five-year-old son and a three-year-old daughter who do not know their Georgia cousins.

I think of others who might reluctantly attend any type of reunion. Will their life challenges and concerns impact their reunion experience? Fear of the unknown and feeling uncomfortable about one's station in life has conquered the hearts and minds of many would-be attenders to family gatherings, to the point of driving them mad or off the beaten path into obscurity. Will I measure up? Am I the apple that doesn't fall far from the tree? What if that apple is sour? What if they like green "Granny Smith" apples and I am only a "Honey Crisp" variety?

Mapping out family dynamics, real or perceived, can blindside the best of intentions. Driving carefully down the road of regret or getting stuck in a pothole full of perilous persona, can keep one awake staring at the starry sky through the moonroof of your old car. You are who you are and nobody can take that away from you, even your own flesh and blood. Dust off the dirt from your shoes, smile, and let the hug-fest begin as you reacquaint yourself with your family.

My quest to find the ancestry of Preston Riley, my 2nd Great Grandfather was fraught with numerous challenges from the beginning. I almost kicked the tires and "called it a day" many times, waiting to find another, new-to-me branch of the family tree to explore. It must be that Riley DNA of "Fortitudine et Prudentia," that gave me the courage to continue taking laps around the speedway track. Take necessary pit stops, to refuel, and to *slow down*. I decided to not be so concerned with winning the race against time or even popularity contests. It was more important to take the scenic route, however long that drive entailed.

CHAPTER 3: TAKING THE SCENIC ROUTE

After researching the various leaves and branches on my family tree nearly every day for the past seven years, I decided that it was time to slow down and take the scenic route of leisurely exploring my lineage. It seemed that driving the racecar of wanting and needing to know everything about everyone who ever lived in my family was clearly not going to happen overnight. Did I share that I am a true "Type A" with a choleric primary and melancholy secondary personality? As my younger sister Natalie, a true Sanguine social butterfly type, put it so lovingly, "You have the worst two personality types combined."

Yes, don't remind me, I thought and was instantly cheered by a bumper sticker that I enjoy: "Lead, Follow, or Get Out of the Way." I owe my driving personality to my determination to get things done and FAST! When I am slowed down by my sad musings of why my life's challenges keep me in neutral, I shift gears back to fifth gear and I am speeding down the "Autobahn" of my destiny to find whatever it is on the road to my future.

During this leisurely drive down memory lane, over the course of two years, I decided that my ancestors were lost to time. I had no more time to spare, let alone change the tires or direction of my research. I cancelled my *Ancestry.com* membership and tried to move on with my life of rearing children and being a homeschooling Mom. My husband Mike and I had converted from Anglicanism to Catholicism and I was deeply studying the lost and newly found-to-me tenants of the Faith. I was only slightly familiar with the concept of Purgatory, where souls go after they die who are not in a pure enough state to go directly to Heaven and receive the Beatific vision of God. As I began to study more about the Holy Souls of Purgatory that could be relegated there for years and years, while in this State of Purification, these Holy Souls are not able to pray for themselves, but they are able to pray for others. The *Catechism of the Catholic Church (CCC)*[26] is a written work containing the basic tenets of the Catholic faith in a question and answer format.

The Catholic Church teaches:

> *We believe that the multitude of those gathered around Jesus and Mary in Paradise forms the Church of heaven, where in eternal blessedness they see God as he is and where they are also, to various degrees, associated with the holy angels in the divine governance exercised by Christ in glory, by interceding for us and helping our weakness by their fraternal concern. (Paul VI, CPG § 29). CCC 1053*

In turn, here on Earth, we can offer prayers and intentions for those Holy Souls for an earlier release or expedited Purification process.

God allows us the opportunity to offer our almsgiving, prayers, sacrifices, corporal and spiritual works of mercy, for the release of the Holy Souls, and to be merciful and to cooperate with His plan for the salvation for all souls. The *Catechism of the Catholic Church* further explains:

> *"This teaching is also based on the practice of prayer for the dead, already mentioned in Sacred Scripture: "Therefore [Judas Maccabeus] made atonement for the dead, that they might be delivered from their sin." From the beginning the Church has honored the memory of the dead and offered prayers in suffrage for them, above all the Eucharistic sacrifice, so that, thus purified, they may attain the beatific vision of God. The Church also commends almsgiving, indulgences, and works of penance undertaken on behalf of the dead:*

> *Let us help and commemorate them. If Job's sons were purified by their father's sacrifice, why would we doubt that*

---

[26] Originally known as The Baltimore Catechism, The *Catechism of the Catholic Church* is arranged in four parts: The Profession of Faith; The Celebration of the Christian Mystery; Life in Christ; Christian Prayer.

*our offerings for the dead bring them some consolation? Let
us not hesitate to help those who have died and to offer our
prayers for them. CCC 1032*

I began to seriously think about my deceased relatives. Where
were they on the other side of the great divide? The more I
thought about who in my family might be in Purgatory, the more I
wanted to find out who my "lost" relatives were to offer prayers for
them. Not knowing all the names on my family tree, so that I
could pray for them, left me feeling anxious, sad, or better yet, in a
state of perpetual melancholy. I *must* find my ancestors. They
NEED my prayers, I thought daily, and thus my quest to navigate
the dark winter days of barren trees gave me direction in my life.

*It is a holy and wholesome thing to pray for the dead,
that they may be loosed from their sins.*[27]

It became a driving force to pray daily for these lost souls and
unearth the unknown relatives lost to an eternity of having a
forgotten existence.

---

[27] 2 Maccabees 12:46; Douay-Rheims Bible; The 1st and 2nd Books of
Maccabees, have always been accepted by the Catholic Church as inspired
and are called "deuterocanonical" to indicate that they are canonical even
though disputed by some, though regarded by Jews and Protestants as
apocryphal, i.e., not inspired Scripture, are not contained in the Jewish list of
books drawn up at the end of the first century.

HOLLY HENDERSON

CHAPTER 4: THE HIGHWAY TO HEAVEN

As I write this chapter, it is Maundy Thursday of Holy Week. Maundy Thursday, the night of the Last Supper and when Jesus washed the feet of his disciples. The last three days of Holy Week are referred to as the Easter or Sacred Triduum (Triduum Sacrum), the trio of events of Christ's redemption: Holy Thursday, Good Friday and Holy Saturday. Holy Thursday is devoted to the institution of the Eucharist, the Christian ceremony commemorating the Last Supper which is "the source and summit of the Christian life."

> *Greater love* hath *no* man *than* this, that a man *lay down* his life for his *friends.* ... The greatest love you can show is to give *your life* for your *friends.*[28]

They say that blood is thicker than water, and this is true. It is also said, that you can pick your friends but you can't pick your family, and this is also true. Sometimes are friends become our family, but even estranged family members cannot separate the genetic bond of DNA that they share. On the cross, Christ said to his Mother Mary, "Behold Your Son, and then to the disciple John, "Behold your mother" (Jn 19:25-27). Even in our Lord's dying moments, he made provision for His Mother to have a family. This was important to Him and family should be important to us despite the difficult and trying situations we will encounter.

> *Bear with each other and forgive one another if any of you has a grievance against someone. Forgive as the Lord forgave you.*[29]

The family is the Domestic Church and the foundation of our

---

[28] John 15:3
[29] Colossians 3:13

society. It is within the family unit, where individuals learn how to interact with others, share, care for others and learn how to love our neighbors as we love ourselves. The passing down of family traditions for Easter and Christmas are the bedrock of the Christian faith.

The faith not only passed from our grandparents and their grandparents over Sunday dinners and amid housework and chores, but from the very forefathers of our faith: the Early Church. It is not only our responsibility to pass on the faith to our children and grandchildren but it is our duty as Christians to go forth and multiply. The Bible commands us to "honor your father and mother, as the Lord your God commanded you, so that you may live long and that it may go well with you in the land the Lord your God is giving you" (Deut 5:16).

The passing on of our faith through the generational bloodline is our Highway to Heaven. The pearly gates of Heaven await the Faithful and the purified members of the Body and family of Christ, and our genetic family members. May it be said of each of us, regardless of the difficulties that life brings us, "But as for me and my house, we will serve the LORD" (Josh 24:15).

CHAPTER 5: THE SCIENCE OF ENGINGEERING

A recent Google search defined engineering as a noun meaning "the branch of science and technology concerned with the design, building, and use of engines, machines, and structures; the work done by, or the occupation of, an engineer; the action of working artfully to bring something about." Merriam-Webster.com further defined engineering as "the work of designing and creating large structures (such as roads and bridges) or new products or systems by using scientific methods; the control or direction of something (such as behavior)."

As a novice genealogist, I really did not think about my family research in the mindset of an engineer, but subconsciously my M.S. in Engineering must have been winding like clockwork to ensure that my actions brought about a desired end of finding my long-lost ancestors. My mind really *did* control the direction research methodology.

Many genetic genealogists will tell you that to select the appropriate DNA test kit that you must first know what research question it is that you trying to solve. If you are looking for answers to the ancestry of your maternal great-grandmother, then you cannot take a male Y-DNA test to solve your inquiry. For instance, if you choose an autosomal DNA (atDNA) test, then you will be left with a mixed bag of answers, literally. As an atDNA test results in a mixture of both your maternal and paternal DNA that is unable to be separated. An atDNA test is likened unto mixing various ingredients to bake a cake. These ingredients include: flour, sugar, eggs, oil, etc.

One is unable to distinguish from the results of an atDNA test whether the sugar and eggs portion represents the maternal line or whether the scoops of flour are from the paternal side. Maybe the two parts of the oil is divided between both sides of the family tree. A maternal mtDNA test is what is needed to clearly answer this research question. What is one to do when they do not know or have access to the needed descendant on a paternal line, like my Riley line, to test for more information?

Sometimes, a researcher is forced to make what would be considered a left-field wild hypothesis. Only time, and the end results, will tell if the hypothesis is correct or not. Thus, this researcher, having only the oral history of the Riley family descendants of Preston Riley to go on, set out to corroborate the passed down oral history with historical documents and online Riley family trees created by unknown and possible distant relatives.

My research question, the one that plagued me in my sleep every night for the past year, was, *"What is the full name of the white Judge who fathered Preston Riley, my second Great Grandfather?"*

To begin my experiment, I used a combination of research methodologies, including: deductive (theory-testing quantitative analysis), inductive (theory-generating qualitative analysis) and empirical (analysis of statistics based on documents).

Step 1: Begin interviewing descendants of Preston Riley.

Sometimes, this first step might seem counter-intuitive to the novice researcher. This means, if you have had many in person conversations with your Great Aunt Thelma or a few phone conversations with your Cousin Edna, then you might believe that you have already "interviewed" them. In fact, you have interviewed them, but *have you interviewed them with your specific research question?*

I called Edna (Edwards) Lucas (my 1st Cousin, twice removed) and began what would be the start of a lovely relationship, even though we live 13 hours away by car. Edna is in her 80s and has a sharp mind and quick wit. She could recall facts as if they were in a textbook and her vivid memories made me feel like her various

childhood incidents happened only yesterday. Dear cousin Edna
began snail-mailing me selected pictures of cousins and funeral
programs from those who had passed on long ago.

Her boxes of care packets included letters and handwritten
notes carefully placed in page protectors; I eagerly awaited the
mailman as though it were payday. I read and scoured every item
for all helpful clues and new (unknown-to-me) detailed
information. The Riley family has declared and strongly believed
that Preston Riley (born only two years after the Civil War ended)
was the son of the white judge from Butler, Taylor County,
Georgia. Preston is Edna's grandfather and she has fond
memories of him.

Step 2: Research the history of the formation of Butler, Taylor County, Georgia.

Again, this step might seem obvious, but honestly, I had never
actually looked up the historical information of the birthplace of
my 2nd great-grandfather. Google proved again to yield a
multitude of research results that I carefully read and re-read. I
found a clue, in the *New Georgia Encyclopedia*, as it gave the
history of Butler; one of its boundaries being the Flint River which
at one time belonged to the Creek Indians. (Little did I know at
the time of reading the article, that Preston Riley's land bordered
the Flint River; his mother Sallie is believed to be and had striking
features of a Native American with her waist-length, straight black
hair and high cheekbones).

The *USGArchives.net* preserved an account of an "A.H. Riley"
who was an Ordinary Court Judge, or one who served as an
overseer of the affairs of the estate of its citizens. (Again, little did
I know at the time, but this A.H. Riley would be an important
figure and clue in my research hypothesis. His age was too young
to fit the description of who could be my possible 3rd great-
grandfather.)

Another search result listed an article of the history of Butler
County which mentioned a "Thomas J. Riley" as an Inferior Court

Justice during the early 1800s.[30] This guy looks promising, I thought. On a whim, I theorized that Thomas J. Riley was the father of Preston Riley.

Step 3: Decide on a theory, of a possible relative, and input that name on your online family tree (with the word "theory" in parenthesis behind the person's surname).

The journey began. I decided to research the family tree of this said, Thomas J. Riley. Who was he? Who are his parents?   His grandparents? What was his affiliation to the forming and naming of Butler, Taylor County, Georgia, where my present-day relatives live?

If you have ever been online reading anything, you eventually come to find out that not everything on the Internet is accurate. This includes the much beloved websites of *Ancestry.com*, *GeniTree.com*, *MyHeritage*, and others.   If there are humans doing data input with their own subjective findings blended with actual objective information, then there will be a vast array of misinformation. (*Gasp. Sigh.*) Oh no, the horror that so-and-so is not really the wife of your maternal 5th Cousin twice removed!

But what is a researcher to do? Once the genealogy bug bites you, you are infected with sleepless nights of researching the infinite number of possibilities that could be the finding that you dream of in those rare moments of sleep. A researcher continues researching, that is what they do!

With the online clues of Thomas J. Riley, a "judge", who helped give the name of the town Butler, I started stalking the Internet

---

[30] Childs, Essie Jones. *They Tarried in Taylor a Georgia County;* Warner: Central Georgia Genealogical Society, 1992; (http://www.rootsweb.ancestry.com/~gataylor/infctmin.htm): accessed 28 April 2016); citing Inferior Court Minutes Book in Probate Judge's Office, Butler, Taylor County, Georgia, Courthouse; entry for Jeremiah Wilchar, Hiram Drain (Drane), T (Thomas) J. Riley, John Sturdivant and Isaac Mulkey presiding, in naming county site of Butler, 18 Feb 1852.

and *Ancestry.com* even more! *Ancestry.com* became my new best
friend. She was available 24/7 and had lots of information to give.
She allowed me to share my thoughts and theories, right or wrong,
and change my mind time and time again.

All she wanted in return was a monthly fee of $19.99 which I
happily paid month after month after month after month. I paid
the fee because I was getting somewhere, anywhere it would take
me. I would pay the toll, pay the piper to pipe me a tune, as I
methodically listened to her tunes and looked through her musical
scripts. But when would this cacophony of information end? I was
becoming a mad composer, an aggressive driver on this "road of
no return."

***Step 4: Realize that your research is wonderful and
possibly life-changing, but that you still need a LIFE
and your loved-ones are the land of the living. Let the
dead rest, they will still be there tomorrow...***

This is a very difficult step in the research process. What do
you mean by "stop and take a break" and get some fresh air? And
oh, yeah, it's time to put your kids to bed (again). Why does the
doorbell ring or your toddler have a blow-out diaper, just as you
are about to uncover the BIGGEST FIND ever? Well, at least the
find of that day, or rather, that hour. Scratch that, make that the
BIGGEST FIND OF THE MINUTE! Apparently, looking for your
long-lost relatives doesn't happen overnight. The more of them
there are to find, the more days it takes to find each one.
(*Seriously? For real?*)

Yes, seriously and very real, even though they have been
deceased for hundreds of years (and for those who are related and
can prove the blood-line to royalty, those blue-bloods have been
dead for centuries)! (*Super sigh.*) For a "type-A" personality like
myself, this research was never and IS never going to end, so I
might as well take time now to smell the roses and not get stung by
bees. Make some lemonade out of those sour lemons mixed with
wild honey from those bees, as this has been a drippy and wild
ride.

Step 5: Sneak back to the computer in the middle of the night when the household is sound (or snoring) asleep. Tap Tap Tap on the keyboard to find your destiny.

This step is on-going, for a lifetime.

Step 6: Try to come to terms that Step 5 will last forever and decide to employ outside help for your quest of quality information.

Reconcile in your mind and your budget after your insomnia from numerous late-night rendezvous with *Ancestry.com*, that it is time to seek help, professional help, from those who care. This step usually involves more time and money and waiting by the computer for an email notification. Wait by the mailbox for a package from your favorite paid research assistant. In my case, I stalked the Internet and *Gedmatch.com* (after I had uploaded my raw DNA results from Family Tree DNA). I began to reach out to distant, new-to-me cousins (that had unfamiliar surnames but shared a common ancestor, that neither of us could identify) to ask a gazillion-and-one questions. A few of them became my new inner circle of confidants who were eager to learn about the other side of our lost family tree.

Step 7: Compile and organize all the documents and information gathered by the team collaboration and interpret the data.

This step requires a great deal of patience and coffee as it will take a long while to complete. Using an online website or mobile app, such as *Evernote*, was vital and valuable to my research. With the *Evernote* app, I could work on multiple devices and could access the information that was saved and catalogued using descriptive meta-tags (i.e. Riley, Preston Riley, NSDAR research, 1870 US Census, September 2016 research, etc.).

I created various folders and stacks that enabled me to quickly find the bevy of collected files and documents. My long-time

steady of *Microsoft Word,* is a tried-and-true resource. Adding
Amazon.com's self-publishing division of *CreateSpace.com's* book
template is allowing me to type this book at this very moment.

Step 8: Consider joining a lineage society that can aid and guide your genealogical research and provide data interpretation.

Data interpretation. What does that even mean? No, seriously.
Who can accurately interpret data that is not biased as a
researcher? I decided that a lineage society, an organization that
exists to promote the research of one's ancestry and preserve one's
findings, was necessary. As a member, if those findings are proved
to be accurate, then your work is verified. Not only can it greatly
aid your research but also make it worthwhile if your theories,
prove to be correct. Thus, I decided to apply to the historic and
prestigious National Society of Daughters of the American
Revolution (NSDAR) lineage society.[31] According to the *DAR.org*
website, to apply to the NSDAR,

*"Any woman 18 years or older who can prove lineal, bloodline
descent from an ancestor who aided in achieving American
independence is eligible to join the NSDAR. She must provide
documentation for each statement of birth, marriage and death,
as well as of the Revolutionary War service of her Patriot
ancestor."*

The NSDAR, established on October 11, 1890, and Incorporated
in 1896 by an Act of Congress, seeks historic preservation,
education and patriotism. Currently there are over 185,000 ladies
who can prove lineal, bloodline descent from a someone who gave
aid or fought in the American Revolutionary War.

I first remember learning about the NSDAR in 4th grade, when
a NSDAR member spoke to my school. An avid history lover and
genealogy enthusiast, I decided that I was up to the task of the
high bar of documenting with original sources, every birth,
marriage and death record for each generation leading back to my

---

[31] The DAR application for Holly Denise Ellison Henderson was mailed
December 15, 2017 and was marked as a "verified" application on March 28,
2017 and approved on April 5, 2017; and induction into the DAR Harmony
Hall Maryland Chapter on April 21, 2017.

Patriot! It clearly must be that dogged determination and bravery imbedded in that part of my Irish DNA, that made me believe that this documentation challenge was possible.

One must have thick skin, very thick skin, when it comes to a lineage society inspecting your work. They will review and interpret the data of what *you* believe are true facts and critique the evidence covering over 240 years of American history. Let that quantitative fact sink in a moment. Can you accurately document over 240 years of lineal descent from somebody who lived and fought during the time of George Washington?

Step 9: Watch documentaries, attend lectures, read genealogy articles, books, blogs. Keep talking to every family member and stranger you know about your research quest to learn new clues of golden nugget information; Employ the latest best practices in your research experiment.

My family interviews proved helpful and valuable. It was also insightful to talk with ladies at church, neighbors, and strangers about my research. These friends and strangers had their own unique stories of similar research quandaries and resource tools that assisted them in finding facts about their family. Their ideas, support, and commentary was encouraging and often gave me the fuel to continue the long road of research.

Step 10: Fill the test tube with collected data, turn the Bunsen burner on to purify the information, and wait for the conclusive results.

Once you have gathered as much information as possible, work with the local linage society genealogist to complete your membership application with your prospective Patriot. Your application will be reviewed by several knowledgeable genealogists who will either, accept your application as is, deny your application, or request additional supplemental evidence for your application. My NSDAR application went through three rounds of scrutiny at the national level before I received a definitive answer.

Building a sturdy structure, like a road or dwelling, requires a combination of the right materials, man power, accurate mathematical calculations and meticulous details, all working simultaneously to create the desired outcome. The same factors are needed to achieve the desired result of "creating a new product (a Rev. War Patriot) or system (of successful genealogical research)," for employing the scientific method of building your family tree. This engineering endeavor, "the action of working artfully to bring something about," is a creative venue and slow process, but one that yields an eternally lasting effect.

CHAPTER 6: THE CROSSROADS

As a Person of Color who is tri-racial, (a mixture of African, Native American, and European descent), searching for one's ancestry can be, *interesting*, to say the least. I often find it comical and annoying, when I am given a "survey" to fill out regarding race and ethnicity. Do I check only one box, some of the boxes, or all of the above boxes? Checking just one box does not seem to genuinely capture the essence of who I am or what I represent.

Searching for your ancestry prior to, during, and after the Civil War era can prove to be especially challenging for a Person of Color. African-Americans were not even listed by name until the 1870 U.S. Federal Census, more than five years after the close of the Civil War. Just because the War ended, did not mean that Persons of Color were treated in a "civil" manner.

It was for this purpose that the U.S. Government created the Freedmen's Bureau to assist newly freed slaves in starting a new life.[32]   Slaves who once slept in the slave quarters were now homeless, jobless and well, still penniless. The Freedmen's Bureau recorded marriages, created bank accounts and heard legal cases of stolen property and mistreatment of non-whites due to the stressful social climate created from prewar and postwar hostilities.

---

[32] "African American Records: Freedmen's Bureau," National Archives and Records Administration; accessed May 22, 2017; https://www.archives.gov/research/african-americans/freedmens-bureau; Established in the War Department in 1865, the Bureau was tasked to begin social and economic reconstruction that would bring freed people of color to full citizenship; providing employment, education and legal representation, issuing food and clothing, locating family members, legalizing marriages, securing abandoned or confiscated lands, securing back pay and pensions, among many other relief efforts.

Certain clues avail themselves to the savvy researcher, if the researcher knows what terms or keywords to look for in early American documents. The first U.S. Federal Census was conducted in 1790.[33] The term "Free Person of Color" is used to indicate, that a non-white person had his freedom and is listed by his name. As compared to the 1860[34] U.S. Census- Slave Schedules where an enslaved black person is only recorded as a *tally mark*, with no name given, listed under the head of the household of the plantation owner.

However, by studying vintage family Bibles, personal letters, newspaper articles, land deeds, wills, and other historical court documents, one can find that the property of slave owners are listed by name, because even though they are not by law considered "persons", they are considered legally taxable and thus need to be properly accounted by the head of the household.

It is in these personal papers or legal documents that one's ancestor is referred to not only by name, but approximate age and by physical description (e.g. "high yellow", "mulatto, "dark skinned with a scar on his leg," etc.). The 1870 U.S. Census[35] is a gold-mine for the person researching potential relatives for the bevy of additional information listed.

Even though this new-found information contained in the 1870 U.S. Census is priceless, it still can only transport you so far back in time. If your 3rd great-grandfather, Joseph Maclin, is listed as "mulatto", living in Mecklenburg County, VA, and being age 40 in 1870, then that gives him an approximate birth year of 1830. But

---

[33] Richard Murphy, "Freedom Road: *An American Family Saga from Jamestown to World War,"* lecture, Daughters of the American Revolution, Harmony Hall Chapter: Maryland, 2017.

[34] See Appendix C; "1860 United States Federal Census – Slave Schedule," database, *Ancestry.com,* (http://search.ancestry.com/cgi-bin/sse.dll?indiv=1&dbid=7668&h=1419926&ssrc=pt&tid=22817676&pid=284394794O3&usePUB=true : accessed 28 April 2016), entry for Thomas J. Riley, "Name of Slave Owner", District 768, Page 17, Southern Division, Taylor County, Georgia.

[35] See Appendix D; "1870 United States Federal Census," database, *Ancestry.com.* (http://www.ancestry.com : accessed 28 April 2016), entry for Preston Riley, Prattsburg, Talbot County, Georgia; citing National Archives microfilm publication M593_175; Page: 91B; Image: 356361; Family History Library Film: 545674.

since 1830 is within the timeframe of not listing an enslaved Person of Color by name, then you are stuck in the early 1800s with not a lot of additional information to continue your search.

The researcher must then decide whether he wants to go down the road of looking for ancestry that made his relative "mulatto." Keep in mind that the term mulatto can be a mixture of the following combinations: White + Black, White + Native American or Black + Native American, or even White + Black + Native American. The researcher has now arrived at *"the crossroads."*

Which way do I go to look for information? Which path of clues or information does one now follow? Do you choose the path of a possible white ancestor first, since there are more documents of the taxable white male, head of household?

Does one follow the clue that a "mulatto" male in Virginia may have been a Free Person of Color who not only owned land but also possibly was a black slaveowner of his own relatives to ensure their wellbeing and keep family ties unbroken? If my Joseph Maclin was Native American, to which tribe did he belong? Spaponi, Creek, Cherokee[36] (as listed on the Dawes Rolls) or a mixture of various tribes? Choosing one racial path to follow can potentially lead to you a dead-end road, cause you to make an annoying U-turn in your methodology, or keep you on an endless road leading to who knows where. I was advised to *"not go on my research path to where you want to go, but go where the document trail leads you"*.

In my research theory, Thomas J. Riley, the wealthy white Judge and slave owner in Taylor County, GA, is the father of my 2ⁿᵈ great-grandfather, Preston Riley. I chose this *"Riley Road"* path to set upon my vehicle of inquiry. I worked both ends of Thomas J. Riley's family tree, searching for hours on end, day after day, month after month.

I was fortunate to find an excerpt of T.J. Riley's family Bible listed in *"A Rockaway in Talbot, Travels in an Old Georgia*

---

[36] See Appendix E, Dawes Rolls also known as the "Final Rolls", are the lists of individuals who were accepted as eligible for tribal membership in the "Five Civilized Tribes": Cherokees, Creeks, Choctaws, Chickasaws, and Seminole.

County," Volume IV, by William H. Davidson.[37] The Bible information, listed on page 207, included the names of the slaves born as property to the Riley family, including a *"Caroline"* born April 22, 1851; a *"Hannah"* born February 10, 1819; and a *"Sallie"* born September 20, 1847, all matching the birth years and names of my ancestors.

T.J. was married to Harriet (Howe), the daughter of Robert Howe and Susanna (Gray) Riley. Harriet is a distant cousin of T.J.'s, who were both the great-granddaughter of Rev. War Patriot Jacob Riley. It appears Harriet died in childbirth on April 5, 1850, and is buried along with eight other Riley family members in the Archibald Gray Family Cemetery according to the Taylor County Historical Genealogical Society.[38]

T.J. Riley, a widower,[39] is listed as having a 12-year-old black female slave in the 1860 Slave Schedule which matches the record of Sallie.[40] In October 1866, T. J. Riley petitions the Ordinary Court, as recorded in the October 1866 Ordinary Court minutes of Taylor County[41], on behalf of "Sallie Riley (freedwoman) and her

---

[37] *A Rockaway in Talbot: Travels in an Old Georgia County*, Volume, William H. Davidson, Page 207, lists the names of the slaves born as property to T.J. Riley.

[38] Taylor County Historical Genealogical Society, Inc.; *Taylor County Tracer*, Vol 14, Issue 9, September 2009; Harriet (Howe) Riley is buried along with two small graves on either side of her and in the family's cemetery. The same Taylor County Tracer edition, page 7, gives additional key information of "African Americans buried in Gray – Harris Cemetery, listing 11 names, including: Anisky Riley, Clinton T. Riley, George Riley, Hattie Riley, Henrietta Riley and Sanders Key (S.K.) Riley

[39] *Cemeteries of Taylor Co Georgia*, by XX indicates that Harriet (Howe) Riley, T.J.'s wife died on April 5, 1850, It appears that T.J. Riley did not remarry as no one who can be considered his spouse is listed on the 1860 and 1870 Census records.

[40] "1860 Slave Schedule," District 768 Southern Division, Taylor Co Georgia, Page 17; According to Aunt Florence's notes Sallie became pregnant at thirteen years of age.

[41] "Taylor County Ordinary Court Minutes, [July 1852-May 1869]," database *Rootsweb.Ancestry.com,* (http://www.rootsweb.ancestry.com/~gataylor/infctmin.htm : accessed 1 May 2017), entry for Thomas Riley, Sallie Riley, William Riley, Tim Riley order, October Term 1866; U.S. Freedmen's Bureau, Ordinary Court, Butler, Taylor County, Georgia; citing Family History Library Roll: 321,092; Page: 215.

two children William and Tim aged 17 years and 3 years 6 months
who are without means of support and education.[42] Preston Riley
was born in 1868, only two years after the Ordinary Court
appearance. His brother, Clinton T. Riley, also the son of Sallie
Riley and T.J. Riley, was born in 1875.[43] The information was
bittersweet, sour with the truth of their enslavement and yet a
sweet research find.

After the Civil War ended, at the time of emancipation, Sallie's
surname is listed as *Riley*. It is purported that T.J. Riley is also
buried, along with sons Clinton and S.K., in the same Archibald
Gray Family Cemetery although no grave marker can be found for
T.J. Riley.[44]

Nearly 14 years after T.J.'s death, Sallie marries John Mangham
in 1908,[45] who becomes the step-father to Sallie's children.[46]

---

[42] Ibid. Thomas Jefferson Riley "requests that they be bound to him until
he is 21...payment of $100 and $50 to be paid to Sallie at the end of
indenture." These court minutes show T.J. Riley's public acknowledgement
and legal concern for Sallie and his biological children.

[43] Seven children were born to T.J. Riley and Sallie Riley.

[44] "U.S., Find A Grave Index, 1600s-Current;" database *FindAGrave.com*,
(http://www.findagrave.com/cgi-
bin/fg.cgi?page=gr&GRid=116693031&ref=acom): accessed 28 April 2016),
entry for Thomas Jefferson Riley. The land where this cemetery is located is
described and further corroborated by the 1979 letter from Frank Riley to
Aunt Florence Riley.

[45] "Georgia, Marriage Records from Select Counties, 1828-1978,"
database, Ancestry.com, (http://www.ancestry.com : accessed 28 April
2016), entry for Sallie Riley and John Mangham, marriage date of 19 Jan
1908, Taylor County, GA.
Both individuals are listed as colored, (c) on this record. Sallie Mangham is
listed as widowed and living in the household of her son Preston and
granddaughters Louvada and Florence in the 1910 Census.

[46] Georgia, State Supreme Court Case Files, Docket 3, no. 12087, Olivia
McCarty v. Sarah Mangham, October 13, 1915; Georgia Archives Record
Group 92-1-1, Record no. A-34818, RCB-9251, Georgia State Archives,
Athens; the children of Sallie Mangham were listed as surname Riley not as
Mangham in Clinton's will dated 27 Dec 1907. In his will, Clinton names "my
mother Sallie Mangham" as "executor" and "my brothers" W.C., Preston, and
S.K. Riley." This will is brought before the Georgia Supreme Court, the Case
of McCarty vs. Mangham. Clinton's widow, Olivia, had remarried Mr.
McCarty, even though the will specifically states if his wife remarries, his
land would revert to his mother and executor of his estate, Sallie (Riley)
Mangham. Sallie won the court case.

As noted earlier, Clinton is buried in the same cemetery as Harriet.

The more I dug, the more information I unearthed, and every inch of soil led me deeper to the root of the family's foundation. The buried treasure trove of lost artifacts included Georgia Superior Court records of wills and land deeds, property tax digests and other probate records, birth certificates, marriage certificates, death certificates, other vintage family Bible transcriptions that have been digitized, historical maps, county histories, and federal census entries.

There is genealogical "meme" about *seeking dead people.* Some folks care about long-forgotten relatives but some folks are focused on the here and now of changing diapers and raising children. After the Resurrection of Jesus, the Angels ask the women, "Why do you seek the living among the dead (Luke 24:5)?" I suppose, if I had this encounter, my reply would have been, "Yes, Christ is the Lord. I need to know who my loved ones are so that I may find them again in Heaven." Until that great and dreadful day of Judgement, one can spend a lifetime, asking others, seeking relatives and knocking on the doors of Eternity.

It is in this lifetime that we seek those from long-ago. We visit cemeteries personally and virtually. We transcribe tombstones, carefully read obituaries, look at family photos, and family Bibles. We remember loved ones in our thoughts and prayers. But mostly, we long for days of old to have a first or last chance encounter with them.

CHAPTER 7: ROADBLOCKS

Traffic jams, diversions, getting lost, and road work are all major road blocks while driving to one's destination. These unnecessary and untimely circumstances cause one anxiety and possible "road rage." Traveling down the road of research can also be frustrating and limit the speed and success of reaching one's destination in a timely and enjoyable manner.

Research road blocks are probably the bane of a genealogist's existence, excuse the pun. We want answers FAST! We want those answers of yesteryear, like yesterday! Why aren't certain records digitized yet? What happened to the 1890 Census? Its disappearance seems more like a carjacking situation or valuable and irreplaceable data. Certain key family members are "missing in action" on records, while other unfamiliar names appear on the list. Who are these (unknown-to-me) people, anyway? Does the matriarch of the family still have the inside cover of the vintage family Bible from 1820 sitting in her attic or on the coffee table? These examples and inquiries are only some of the pebbles hurled at your windshield while traveling down the path of patience and persistence.

The researcher *must* journey on, despite a missing map of details and lack of a direction to reach one's destination.

My late-night encounters with *Ancestry.com*, early morning transcriptions of fantastic but forgotten family ledgers, and mid-day readings of memoirs and mementoes were both magnetic and maddening. Day after endless day, document after endless document, left me seeing stars and blind to the time passing through the hourglass.

The biggest boulders to stand in my path of forward research motion were:

- Time (there is never enough)

- Daily household chores (laundry piling up like "Mt. Washmore")

- Money (there is always some subscription service or book, old or new, that promises to help break down those "brick walls")

- Records (that have not *yet* been digitized or *worse* that don't exist)

- Travel (to and fro and to and fro, both in your mind and in your vehicle, going somewhere, yet, nowhere)

- Desire (wanting data that you cannot find)

Specifically, I had great difficulty navigating the pre- and post-Civil War era records of Preston Riley and his mother. Preston was born only three years after the close of the Civil War. A Freedmen's Bureau record, initially found online, gives an accounting of Sallie and Thomas Jefferson Riley with the two older brothers of Preston, Tim, and William, before the Taylor County Ordinary Court. But could I prove that Tim and William were the sons of Mr. Riley? Could I prove that the land from McCarty vs. Mangham was the land that Mr. Riley gave to Sallie, a former enslaved woman, and their offspring? Could I prove that Jacob and John Riley lived in Orange County, North Carolina, during the late 1700s?

It was a great discovery to finally find evidence of both proof of residence and proof of service that my 6th great-grandfather, Jacob Riley, "rendered material aid" to the Continental Army during the Revolutionary War. That part was easy. Apparently, the forefathers and mothers of this nation kept meticulous records that have survived intact and carefully preserved in the sands of time.

My biggest roadblock was in proving the father-son relationship between Thomas Jefferson Riley and Preston Riley. I was on a mission and a mandate left unfinished by other Riley relatives to *"bridge the gap"* of information.

CHAPTER 8: BRIDGING THE GREAT DIVIDE

Have you ever been afraid to drive across a bridge towering
over a large body of water?   Here in Maryland, thousands of
people drive over the famous Bay Bridge daily.   This 5-mile
vehicular crossing connects Maryland's western and eastern
shores of the Chesapeake Bay. In its early days, the bridge was the
world's longest continuous over-water steel structure. Currently,
it is actually known as one of the "world's scariest bridges![47]

I have driven over the Bay Bridge a few times travelling to
Ocean City, Maryland, for beach vacations.   Yes, I can indeed
testify that this bridge is so scary for some drivers, that they stop
before approaching the bridge, and even pay other persons to
drive them across to the other side of the bridge.[48] Fortunately for
me, my husband Mike is a brave and excellent chauffer.

While most people might have their first thoughts of defining a
bridge as "a structure carrying a road across a river," it can also be
used to bypass an obstacle. Also, a bridge is something that can
form a connection between two things. As a communications
employee for the Maryland Department of Transportation
(MDOT), it was my duty when first hired to study all the modes of
transportation handled by MDOT.   Planes,   trains,   and
automobiles, yes, of course. Even buses, boats, highways, and bi-
ways, and of course, bridges. In the realm of public affairs, being
the liaison to the media and the public to ensure accurate

---

[47] "Fun Facts about the Chesapeake Bay Bridge," *Hola Blog*, published
on November 7, 2014, accessed May 22, 2017,
 http://www.holabirdsports.com/blog/fun-facts-about-the-chesapeake-bay-
bridge/.
[48] "Don't look down! The Maryland bridge so terrifying locals pay $25
to be driven across in their own car," by Helen Pow; Daily Mail Online;
published on May 29, 2013 and accessed May 22, 2017;
 http://www.dailymail.co.uk/news/article-2331679/Chesapeake-Bay-bridge-
The-Maryland-bridge-terrifying-locals-pay-25-company-shuttle-car.html.

information is disseminated in a timely manner can be quite challenging. The information that you give becomes public record. As the spokesperson, you are being quoted to go on this public record. It is even more important if one wants to be a public affairs specialist, who effectively bridges between the government agency and all its stakeholders.

I suppose it was the MDOT training ground and previously being a "cross-trained" airline employee (ticket agent, gate agent, ramp agent, and eventually flight attendant), that I learned how to specialize in effectively communicating and being a bridge to the public. Anyone in a customer service capacity knows that while it may be the implied company policy of the "customer is always right" (on the surface), the customer is sometimes wrong (beneath the surface). However, one must be poised and tactful enough to provide and resolve situations and sometimes confrontations.

Investigating facts and myths of one's family tree also requires the same type of effective communication to retrieve said data, connect missing pieces of information that will provide a sound research foundation, and often to be a bridge of reconciliation for unveiled family secrets and truths. Ignorance is not always bliss!

A prudent researcher will tackle hard and controversial information with the utmost care and consideration. Should I share with relatives that our great Aunt Sarah placed a child for adoption? Did 5th Great-Grandpa Tony have his land confiscated because he didn't pay his taxes? What if, the research shows the exciting find, of that elusive 4th great-grandparent who fought in the Civil War? Depending on whether he sided with the blue or the gray can elicit an unexpected display of emotion from your living grandparent.

It is in this very context, of a Civil War era find in the Southern state of Georgia, that I, a mixed-race person, found myself juxtaposed between varying sides of history. My 3rd great-grandfather, T.J. Riley, was the wealthiest white plantation owner in Butler, Taylor County, Georgia.[49] Sallie Riley, the mother of

---

[49] *They Tarried in Taylor,* by Essie Childs, listed a few of the 1852 tax receipts from when Taylor Co was formed; entry for "Riley, Thomas J. 23 1/2 slaves, 699 acres, $25,468 value." This would have made him among the richest land owners in the County!

T.J.'s mixed-race children, was a former slave on his plantation. How did Preston Riley[50], a product of a mixed-race union come to fruition? Was T.J.'s relationship with Sallie consensual or forced (as what many folks probably assume)? Do the details of the situation change the fact that I am a descendant of what happened nearly 150 years ago? As I interviewed black Riley relatives, young and old, I received their version of history as what was handed down to them.

Some of the story information went from one extreme to the other, including:

- T.J. Riley was told by his family that he "could be with" this black woman, but not legally marry her. Therefore, he took his inheritance and ran off with this black woman."
- T.J. Riley was so wealthy that it did not matter what his family said, he did what he wanted.
- T.J. Riley ran off with Sallie; they might have "jumped the broom"[51] and lived with his black progeny and that is why his grave has never been found[52].
- Preston was not bi-racial but really a white man.[53]

---

[50] See Appendix F, photograph of Preston Riley, age 70, circa 1938; It is interesting to see that he is enumerated as Black in all census records, and not mulatto, especially when looking at his family picture of having fair skin.

[51] The earliest use of the phrase is in the 1764 English edition of a French work describing a runaway couple hastily making "a *marriage on the cross of the sword*". The English translation rendered the phrase as "*performed the marriage ceremony by leaping over a broomstick*". The phrase is more commonly associated with enslaved blacks, forbidden by law to marry, as an African custom of tying the knot before friends and family.

[52] Although, the date of death of Thomas J. Riley is listed on a newer headstone for his wife, Harriet (Howe) Riley, it is unusual that a wealthy man of his stature and prominence as an Ordinary Judge, and well known in the community, does not have an obituary, specific date of death, or an actual grave that can be located.

[53] "1920 United States Federal Census," database, *Ancestry.com*. (http://www.ancestry.com : accessed 28 April 2016), entry for Lunada Ellison, age 22, mulatto, Militia District 1701, Worth County, Georgia; Roll: T625_286; Page: 13B; Enumeration District: 153; Image: 364; citing Fourteenth Census of the United States, 1920. (NARA microfilm publication T625, 2076 rolls), Washington, D.C. Louvenia/Louvada Riley, his daughter is listed as Mulatto in the 1920 Worth Co, GA census in the household of the

It was my research goal to set out and corroborate the oral family history with documentation. Once the identity of the white Judge, Thomas Jefferson Riley was discovered in the formation of Taylor, County, Georgia, the puzzle pieces started to fit together to form a beautiful mosaic of the hidden paternal lineage of Preston Riley. Many of the research findings presented here have shown to be independently proven by contemporary records.

It is based on all the research that the biological father of Preston Riley was his mother's former owner, T.J. Riley, the descendant of Rev. War Patriots John Riley[54] and Jacob Riley. Jacob Riley, a man from Orange County, North Carolina,[55] who "rendered material aid" to the Continental Army,[56] and a man that I am proud to say, is my 6th great-grandfather.

---

spouse, John Ellison.

[54] "North Carolina, Orange County; *Revolutionary Army War Accounts Vol VI,*" page 524; entry for John Riley.

[55] "North Carolina, Orange County, Hillsborough Wills and Probate Records," Will Book D, page 365, entry for Jacob Riley provides date of birth; "North Carolina, Orange County, Hillsborough Wills and Probate Records," Wills, Volume 5, page 2, entry for Jacob Riley provides date of death as 31 Aug 1812, Orange County, North Carolina.

[56] "North Carolina, Orange County, North Carolina; *Revolutionary War Pay Vouchers,* Roll No S, 115, 120.

CHAPTER 9: CELEBRATING THE JOURNEY

I am the middle daughter of Willi Ellison, the granddaughter of the late William Clifford Ellison ("WC/Ralph"), the great-granddaughter of Louvenia (Riley) Ellison and the 2nd great-granddaughter of Preston Riley.

Like many people, seeking to find relatives lost to history, I have been on a serious quest to solve the elusive mystery of the full name of "The Judge/The Mayor of Butler, Taylor County, Georgia" who was Preston's father and living in the time of the Civil War. It has been a seven-year journey building out my full family tree on *Ancestry.com* and a very intense research effort over the past nine months (just enough time to give birth to the new-found information).

The father of Preston Riley is Judge Thomas Jefferson (T.J.) Riley born in 1811 in Talbot County, GA, and died in 1870. T.J. Riley was an Ordinary Judge in Taylor County (meaning he handled the estate/wills/land deeds for the county residents). His younger half-brother, Alexander Hamilton (A.H.) Riley, also an Ordinary Judge, is the great-grandfather of Frank Riley, the gentleman "who wrote the handwritten letter" to my 2nd great-aunt Florence (Riley) Edwards McHelen in the early 1970s; this is "the letter" that is often referred to in family conversations.

Among other golden nuggets of information on this research path was uncovering the name of Preston's 2nd great-grandfather, Jacob Riley, from Orange Co, NC, that "rendered material aid" to the Continental Army during the Revolutionary War. John Riley, Preston's great-grandfather and son of Jacob,[57] gave patriotic service in that War at the age of 18 in North Carolina.

---

[57] "Georgia, Talbot County Record of Account Book," Book A, 1829, Ordinary Court, Talbot County, Georgia, page 129; entry for Jhon P. Riley, Taylor County, Georgia, 1829.

It is this information that led me to apply and recently be accepted and inducted into the National Society of Daughters of the American Revolution (NSDAR), Harmony Hall Maryland Chapter. To apply to the NSDAR, one must be able to show direct lineal descent providing records for every birth, marriage and death for *every* generation from the applicant to the Patriot, someone who helped the cause for American Independence. Someone heroic who has withstood the test of time.

Jacob Riley begot John Riley.

John Riley begot Joseph Riley.

Joseph Riley begot Thomas Jefferson Riley.

Thomas Jefferson Riley begot Preston Riley.

Preston Riley begot Louvenia (Riley) Ellison.

Louvenia (Riley) Ellison begot William Clifford Ellison.

William Clifford Ellison begot Willi Ellison.

Willi Ellison begot Holly (Ellison) Henderson.

Holly (Ellison) Henderson begot Michael "Paul", Preston Riley and Phoebe Marie Henderson.

This is my story. This is my lineage. This is my family legacy. This is American History.

Riley Road

Traveling down Riley Road
Looking for my lost abode
Yes, I have no doubt
That my Ancestors are calling out
Like Genetic Morse code tapping on my heart
Even though we are miles apart
It is loud and clear
These voices that I hear
I cannot deny
The tears in my eyes
As I pine away
Looking desperately every day
To find them
To find me
For it is me that I seek
In the depths of the deep
Walking, running, driving there
It is a heavy load that I bear
On this lonely stretch of road
That Generations before me sowed
Now it is time to reap
Tears of joy in a timeless feast
The smiley Rileys are my kin
My face is radiant as I grin
Generations past foretold
That I would come home on Riley Road

BIBLIOGRAPHY

Census. 1779. U.S. North Carolina. Orange County. North Carolina State Archives.

Census. 1780. U.S. North Carolina. Orange County. North Carolina State Archives.

Census. 1790. U.S. North Carolina. Orange County. Database. *Ancestry.com,* http://www.ancestry.com : 2016.

Census. 1820. U.S. Georgia. Greene County. Database. *Ancestry.com,* http://www.ancestry.com : 2016.

Census. 1830. U.S. Georgia. Greene County. Database. *Ancestry.com,* http://www.ancestry.com : 2016. Film: 0007037; citing "1830 United States Federal Census."

Census. 1830. U.S. Georgia. Talbot County, Burks. Database. *Ancestry.com,* http://www.ancestry.com : 2016.

Census. 1840. U.S. Georgia. Talbot County. Database. *Ancestry.com,* http://www.ancestry.com : 2016.

Census. 1850. U.S. Georgia. Talbot County. Database. *Ancestry.com,* http://www.ancestry.com : 2016.

Census. 1850. U.S. Georgia. Talbot County, Slave Schedule. Database. *Ancestry.com,* http://www.ancestry.com : 2016

Census. 1860. U.S. Georgia. Taylor County, Militia District 768. Database. *Ancestry.com,* http://www.ancestry.com : 2016.

Census. 1870. U.S. Georgia. Talbot County, Prattsburg. Database. *Ancestry.com.* http://www.ancestry.com : 2016.

Census. 1870. U.S. Georgia. Taylor County, Carsonville. Database. *Ancestry.com,* http://www.ancestry.com : 2016.

Census. 1880. U.S. Georgia. Talbot County, Carsonville. Database. *Ancestry.com*. http://www.ancestry.com : 2016.

Census. 1880. U.S. Georgia. Taylor County, Carsonville. Database. *Ancestry.com,* http://www.ancestry.com : 2016.

Census. 1900. U.S. Georgia. Talbot County, Carsonville. Database. *Ancestry.com*. http://www.ancestry.com : 2016.

"Census. 1900. U.S. Georgia. Taylor County, Carsonville. Database. *Ancestry.com,* http://www.ancestry.com : 2016.

Census. 1910. U.S. Georgia. Talbot County, Carsonville. Database. *Ancestry.com*. http://www.ancestry.com : 2016.

Census. 1910. U.S. Georgia. Taylor County, Carsonville. Database. *Ancestry.com,* http://www.ancestry.com : 2016.

Census. 1920. U.S. Georgia. Talbot County, Carsonville. Database. *Ancestry.com*. http://www.ancestry.com : 2016.

Census. 1920. U.S. Georgia. Taylor County, Carsonville. Database. *Ancestry.com,* http://www.ancestry.com : 2016.

Census. 1930. U.S. Georgia. Talbot County, Carsonville. Database. *Ancestry.com*. http://www.ancestry.com : 2016.

Census. 1930. U.S. Georgia. Taylor County, Carsonville. Database. *Ancestry.com,* http://www.ancestry.com : 2016.

Childs, Essie Jones. *They Tarried in Taylor (a Georgia County).* Warner: Central Georgia Genealogical Society, 1992.

Crilley, Virginia. *Taylor County, GA – Bios Riley, Thomas J.* (http://www.usgwarchives.net/ga/gafiles.htm : accessed 1 May 2017); citing USGenWeb Archives Special Projects.

Davidson, William H. *A Rockaway in Talbot, Travels in an Old Georgia County, Vol IV*. West Point: Hester Printing, 1990.

Davidson, William H. *A Rockaway in Talbot, Travels in an Old Georgia County, Vol IV*. West Point, Georgia: Hester Printing,

1990; Library of Congress Catalog Card Number: 82-73351. Pages, 185, 190-192, 196-198, 207-208.

Delaware. Wilmington. *The Records of Holy Trinity Old Swedes Church*; 1757.

The Catechism of the Catholic Church.
http://www.usccb.org/beliefs-and-teachings/what-we-believe/catechism/index.cfm accessed : May 8, 2017.

The Chicago Manual of Style. 16th edition. Chicago: University of Chicago Press, 2010.

Futhey and Cope. *History of Chester County PA,* published 1881;
http://rootsweb.ancestry.com/~pacheste/Chester.

Georgia. *Compiled Census and Census Substitutes Index, 1790-1890.* Database. *Ancestry.com,* http://www.ancestry.com : 2016

Georgia. *Death Index, 1919-1998.* Database. *Ancestry.com,*
http://www.ancestry.com : 2016.

Georgia. Greene County. Property Tax Digests, 1793-1892.

Georgia. *Marriages, 1699-1944.* Database. *Ancestry.com,*
http://www.ancestry.com : 2016

Georgia. *Marriage Records from Select Counties, 1828-1978.*
Database. *Ancestry.com,* http://www.ancestry.com : 2016.

Georgia. *Property Tax Digests, 1793-1892.* Database.
Ancestry.com, http://www.ancestry.com : 2016.

Georgia. *Returns of Qualified Voters and Reconstruction Oath Books,* 1867-1869. Database. *Ancestry.com,*
http://www.ancestry.com : 2016.

Georgia. *State Supreme Court of Georgia. McCarty v. Mangham,* Record no. A-34818, Georgia State Archives, Athens.

Georgia. Talbot County. Wills and Probate Records, 1742-1992.

Georgia. Taylor County. Freedmen's Bureau Minutes, Ordinary Court, July 1852-May 1869.

Georgia. Taylor County. *Ordinary Court Record of Account Book.* Georgia. Taylor County. *Wills and Probate Records, 1742-1992.*

Georgia. *Wills and Probate Records, 1742-1992.* Database. *Ancestry.com,* http://www.ancestry.com : 2016.

Hay, G.L. and Stewart, M.C. *Cemeteries of Taylor Co Georgia,* page 75. Warner Robins Georgia: Central Georgia Genealogical Society, Inc., 1990.

Helmers, Lois. *Early Records of Greene County, Georgia.* Canal Winchester: Badgley Publishing Co., 2014; page 51, 64-65.

Holabird Sports. *Hola Blog.* http://www.holabirdsports.com/blog/fun-facts-about-the-chesapeake-bay-bridge : accessed 22 May 2017.

International Society of Genetic Genealogy. (https://isogg.org/wiki/Genetic_genealogy : accessed 2 May 2017.

Maryland Transit Administration. *About the Maryland Transit Administration,"* accessed 2 May 2017, https://mta.maryland.gov/about-mta.

McHelen, Florence Riley. Handwritten family notes. Taylor County, Georgia, 1970.

Mills, Elizabeth Shown. *Evidence! Citation & Analysis for the Family Historian.* Baltimore: Genealogical Publishing Co., 1997; revised, 20th printing, 2014.

North Carolina. Hillsborough, Orange County. Will Book D.

North Carolina. *Revolutionary Army War Accounts Vol VI,* p 524.

North Carolina. *Revolutionary War Pay Vouchers,* Roll No S, 115, 120.

Pow, Helen. *Daily Mail Online.*
http://www.dailymail.co.uk/news/article-2331679/Chesapeake-
Bay-bridge-The-Maryland-bridge-terrifying-locals-pay-25-
company-shuttle-car.html : 2017.

Riley, Alexander Hamilton, *Bible Records.* Family pages only.
Online transcription by Pat Richardson.
http://files.usgwarchives.net/ga/talbot/bibles/alexande88bb.txt
: 2016.

Riley-Edwards Family History. Riley-Edwards Family
Reunion program, St. Augustine, Florida, 2015.

Riley, Frank. Handwritten letter to Florence Riley McHelen,
daughter of Preston Riley. Taylor County, Georgia, 1979.

Riley, Joseph, Bible Records. Family pages only. Photocopy held
by unknown source. Online transcription by Pat Richardson.
http://files.usgwarchives.net/ga/taylor/bibles/rileyjos85bb.txt :
2016.

Taylor Co Family Churches. Database. *Rootsweb,*
http://www.rootsweb.ancestry.com/~gataylor/antibp.htm: 2017.
U.S., Find A Grave Index, 1600s-Current. Database
FindAGrave.com, http://www.findagrave.com

APPENDIX A

FIRST RILEY REUNION PROGRAM COVER, 1979

APPENDIX B

LETTER FROM FRANK RILEY, CIRCA 1979

sometime in 1970's or 50's

PAGE (1)

TO: FLORENCE Mc HELEN   SUNDAY — JULY 14,
(DAUGHTER OF PRESS RILEY — TAYLOR COUNTY, GA.)   BUTLER, GA

Dear Florence,

I enjoyed the visit over the telephone with you Sunday & recalling the days of the lifetime of your father, Press Riley.

I have fond memories of him, as I was a young boy at that time. I still think of him & his family often as I pass the homesite on my way to Thomaston, Ga., overlooking the beautiful Flint River. It was located right at the Flint River Bridge on the Taylor County side on U.S. Highway 19 in the northern part of the County.

I can remember what the house where you lived as a child looked like as if I had seen it this morning. It was a house with a front porch all the way across the front with board & batten planks running up & down on the outside.

There was plenty of open land around the house for the growing of crops and vegetables, as your father was a good provider for his family.

You can tell all of your children, grandchildren, great grandchildren, & great-great grandchildren that they have a good heritage, as the Riley Clan were well respected & were good solid citizens in the community.

Press Riley was quite a character and I have fond memories of him as a young boy in happy summer days here on the farm where I live now on a high bluff overlooking the same Flint River (about 2 miles up the River from your former home).

PAGE (2)

Press had a good sense of humor and didn't ever seem to "meet a stranger".

He liked to grow things and I remember my father, Harley Riley, asking him one day at the end of a corn harvest season if he had made a good corn crop and he immediately answered, "I made so much corn that I had to move it off the field to stack it". He never lacked for an answer!

Press thought a lot of my father and we all thought a lot of him.

He liked to walk (as there were very few cars), and about this time of the year when his crop was "laid by" and our crop too, we would look up and would see Press coming to visit us on the farm and we would have a pleasant visit and "catch up on all the news in the community. He would then visit throughout the community.

I remember Judy, his wife, and she was a great support to him and the rest of the family. A man can only do so much for a family, but it takes the support of a good wife and mother, she was this to her family.

Press lived thru the Depression years of the Nineteen twenties & thirties when nobody had much money but the people on the farm faired better than those in the cities and the "pace of life" was much slower in those days, which you and I agreed on the telephone. We could use some of that in today's living!

I wish I had a snapshot picture of Press but no one took many pictures in those days,

Page (3)

I remember his brothers, Keith, Clinton and others, Fay Riley, Doug Riley, Howard Riley, Jess Riley, Will Riley & Homer Riley — all good friends of ours. Some of them were farmers and the others in the timber industry.

Well, Florence, I hope this gives your folks a picture of your father's life and the times in which he lived.

Hope this finds you well and enjoy your family reunion.

Sincerely —
Frank Riley
(Son of Harley Riley)

APPENDIX C

1860. U.S. CENSUS, SLAVE SCHEDULE, TALBOT CO GA

APPENDIX D

1870. U.S. CENSUS, TALBOT CO GA

SCHEDULE 2—Slave Inhabitants in 768 _____ in the County of _____ State of _Georgia_ , enumerated by me, on the _____ day of _July_ , 1860. _____ Ass't Marshal.

APPENDIX E

CHEROKEE NATION, CHEROKEE ROLL - DAWES ROLL, 1868

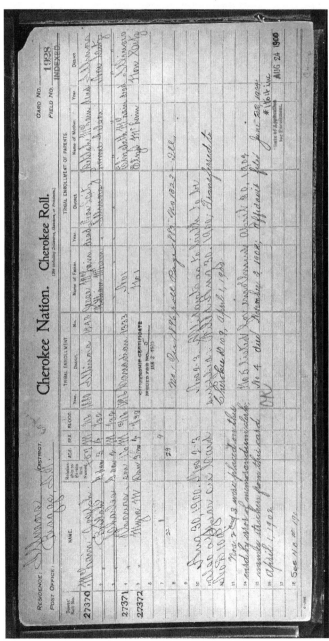

APPENDIX F
PHOTO, PRESTON RILEY, AGE 70

PRESTON RILEY - AGE SEVENTY (When picture taken)

APPENDIX G
ANTIOCH BAPTIST CHURCH CEMETARY,
BUTLER, TAYLOR COUNTY, GEORGIA

This statement was taken from the minutes of The Antioch Baptist Church, "Saturday, October 20, 1867, conference moved that a committee of five brethren be appointed, 3 colored and 2 white, to help the clerk, W.J.F. Mitchell, to draw up letters of dismissal for the purpose of being constituted into a separate church for 'our colored brethren'. Thus, Antioch Baptist Church for people of color was organized in 1869."

Louvenia Riley Ellison   *Sarah Mae "Sally" Riley*

APPENDIX H

U.S. History Timeline

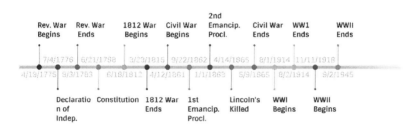

1775-1945

APPENDIX I

Riley Family Timeline

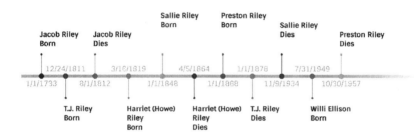

Jacob Riley Born — 12/24/1811
Jacob Riley Dies — 3/16/1819
Sallie Riley Born — 4/5/1864
Preston Riley Born — 1/1/1878
Sallie Riley Dies — 7/31/1949
Preston Riley Dies

1/1/1733 — 8/1/1812 — 1/1/1848 — 1/1/1868 — 11/9/1934 — 10/30/1957

T.J. Riley Born
Harriet (Howe) Riley Born
Harriet (Howe) Riley Dies
T.J. Riley Dies
Willi Ellison Born

1733-1957

APPENDIX J

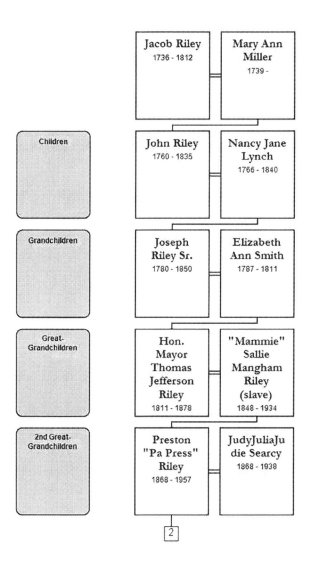

Jacob Riley 1736 - 1812	**Mary Ann Miller** 1739 -
John Riley 1760 - 1835	**Nancy Jane Lynch** 1766 - 1840
Joseph Riley Sr. 1780 - 1850	**Elizabeth Ann Smith** 1787 - 1811
Hon. Mayor Thomas Jefferson Riley 1811 - 1878	**"Mammie" Sallie Mangham Riley (slave)** 1848 - 1934
Preston "Pa Press" Riley 1868 - 1957	**JudyJuliaJudie Searcy** 1868 - 1938

Children

Grandchildren

Great-Grandchildren

2nd Great-Grandchildren

2

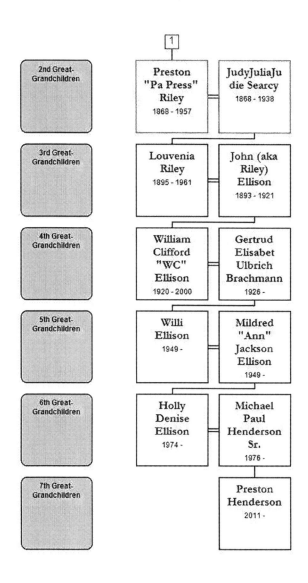

APPENDIX K

Jacob Riley married Mary Ann Miller on 24 Oct 1757, in the Old Swede's Church, Wilmington, Delaware.

Jacob Riley "rendered material aid" to the Continental Army under the North Carolina banner. These are his pay stubs.

ABOUT THE AUTHOR

Six-time national Telly Award Winner Holly Ellison Henderson is a seasoned 20-year public affairs specialist and speechwriter, having served as a Maryland political appointee for both Republican and Democratic Governors. A descendant of Revolutionary War Patriots, preachers, teachers, authors, farmers, moonshiners, and famous rabbis, politics and religion are in her DNA.

She adores alliteration, genetic genealogy, marvelous monograms, and has totally traveled as an international flight attendant. She holds a B.A. in Communications and an M.S. in Transportation Engineering: useful in building bridges of reconciliation and digging out her family tree. Holly is a proud member of the National Society Daughters of the American Revolution (NSDAR) and is studying to be a Third Order Lay Dominican (OP).

Holly and her husband share their home in Southern Maryland with three extraordinary children who enjoy talk radio. Visit her website, TheMessengerMom.com, to sign up for emails where she delivers the Good News message for your life and home.

Made in the USA
Middletown, DE
10 July 2018